W9-BGG-761

GO HOG WILD!

Make Me Laugh!

GO HOG WILD!
jokes from down on the farm

by Peter & Connie Roop / pictures by Joan Hanson

Lerner Publications Company · Minneapolis

To D.R., who inspired our pun-play

Copyright © 1984 by Lerner Publications Company

All rights reserved. International copyright secured.
No part of this book may be reproduced in any form whatsoever
without permission in writing from the publisher except for
the inclusion of brief quotations in an acknowledged review.

Library of Congress Cataloging in Publication Data

Roop, Peter.
  Go hog wild!

  (Make me laugh!)
  Summary: A collection of riddles about farming and
farm animals, including "What do Hawaiian cows wear?"
("moo-moos") and "What does a farmer plow but never
plant?" ("snow").
  1. Agriculture—Anecdotes, facetiae, satire, etc.
2. Wit and humor, Juvenile. [1. Farm life—Wit and
humor. 2. Domestic animals—Wit and humor. 3. Riddles]
I. Roop, Connie. II. Hanson, Joan, ill. III. Title.
IV. Series.
PN6231.A44R66 1984   818'.5402   84-5662
ISBN 0-8225-0982-2 (lib. bdg.)

Manufactured in the United States of America

  2 3 4 5 6 7 8 9 10 93 92 91 90 89 88 87 86 85

Q: How does a farmer get his hogs to market?
A: In a pig-up truck.

Q: What has ears but cannot hear?
A: A field of corn.

Q: What did the chicken say when she threw
an egg at the farmer?
A: The yolk's on you!

Q: When is a pig like ink?
A: When it's in a pen.

Q: What do Hawaiian cows wear?
A: Moo-moos.

Q: Why couldn't the farmer's horse run?
A: It was stalled.

Q: What did the farmer say when he picked
the corn?
A: "Aw, shucks!"

Q: What made the vegetable farmer so rich?
A: His celery was so high.

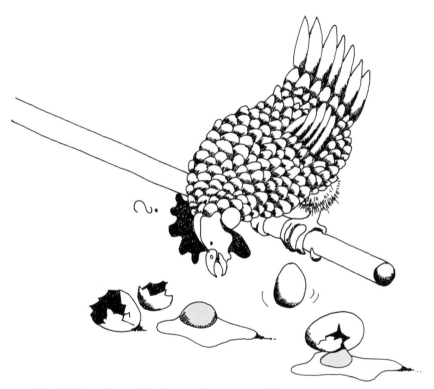

Q: Why do chickens lay eggs?

A: If they dropped them, the eggs would break!

Q: When is a dog's tail like a farmer's cart?
A: When it's a-waggin'.

Q: What's a cow's favorite food?
A: Cow chow.

Q: How does a farmer keep a horse out of a thunderstorm?
A: He pulls in its reins (rains).

First Farmer: I made a scarecrow so terrible
it scared every single crow off my farm.

Second Farmer: That's nothing. My scarecrow
is so awful that the crows brought back the
corn they stole last year!

Q: What do you call a funny horse?
A: A silly filly.

Q: What does a farmer plow but never plant?
A: Snow.

Q: What does a farmer get when his cows eat peanuts?
A: Peanut butter.

Q: Why did the farmer ride his horse to town?
A: It was too heavy to carry.

Q: Why are goats so funny?
A: Because they're always kidding around.

First Pig: It sure is hot!
Second Pig: I know. I'm bacon!

Q: Why is a wild horse so rich?
A: Because he has lots of bucks.

Q: Why was the farmer so famous?
A: He was outstanding in his field.

Q: What do you call an inexpensive chick?
A: A cheap cheep!

Q: What kind of bird can eat a barn in one bite?
A: A barn swallow.

Q: Why didn't the horse eat more hay?
A: He still had a bit in his mouth.

Q: What kinds of keys won't unlock doors?
A: Don-keys and tur-keys.

Q: Where does a farmer keep his young corn?
A: In a corn crib!

Q: What do you call a pony with a sore throat?
A: A hoarse horse.

Q: Why didn't the farmer tell secrets in his field?
A: Because the corn had ears and the wind whispered.

Q: Why was the farmer's horse so lucky?
A: Because it had four horseshoes!

Q: What do you call a sleeping bull?
A: A bull-dozer.

Q: Why was the chicken always in trouble?
A: It used fowl language.

Q: What do you call a skinny horse?
A: A bony pony!

Q: What do cows put on their hamburgers?
A: Moo-stard and cow-chup.

Q: Why did the farmer let his pigs loose
in the woods?

A: He wanted them to go hog wild!

Q: Why did the horse have trouble sleeping?
A: She kept having night-mares.

Q: How does a cow do its math?
A: With a cow-culator!

Q: What's a farmer's favorite sport?
A: Fencing.

Q: Why did the farmer plant eggs?
A: He wanted to grow eggplant.

Q: Why is Santa Claus like a farmer?
A: They both like to hoe, hoe, hoe.

Q: What did the pig squeal when the farmer grabbed him by the tail?
A: "This is the end of me!"

Q: Why did the horse put on a blanket?
A: He was a little colt.

Q: Where does a lamb get a haircut?
A: In a baa-baa shop!

Q: What does a farmer grow if he works very, very hard?

A: Very, very tired!

Q: Why are a farmer's legs like a cow?

A: They both have calves.

Q: What kind of toes do farmers plant?

A: Pota-toes and toma-toes.

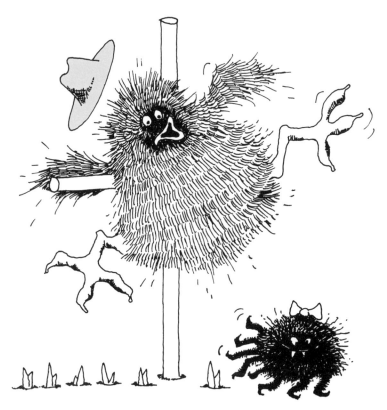

Q: When is a crow a chicken?
A: When it's a scared-crow.

Q: What do you call a young calf?
A: A new moo.

Q: Why did the farmer take a hammer to bed?
A: Because he wanted to hit the hay!

Q: What do you call a cow barn on a holiday?
A: A merry dairy.

Q: Where do cows like to go on Saturday nights?
A: To the moo-vies!

Q: What do well-dressed pigs wear to dinner?
A: Pigs-ties.

ABOUT THE AUTHORS

PETER AND CONNIE ROOP have shared jokes with their students in the United States and Great Britain for the past 11 years. When not joking around, Peter writes historical articles and stories for children, and Connie writes for educational journals. Traveling, camping, and reading with their son, Sterling, are their favorite pastimes. Both graduates of Lawrence University, the Roops now live in Appleton, Wisconsin.

ABOUT THE ARTIST

JOAN HANSON lives with her husband and two sons in Afton, Minnesota. Her distinctive, deliberately whimsical pen-and-ink drawings have illustrated more than 30 children's books. Ms. Hanson is also an accomplished weaver. A graduate of Carleton College, Hanson enjoys tennis, skiing, sailing, reading, traveling, and walking in the woods surrounding her home.

Make Me Laugh!